Cities

Claire Llewellyn

Illustrated by
Roger Stewart

Heinemann

Contents

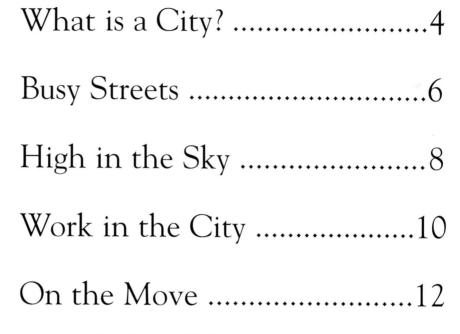

First published in Great Britain in 1998 by Heinemann Library,
Halley Court, Jordan Hill, Oxford, OX2 8EJ,
a division of Reed Educational & Professional Publishing Ltd.
Heinemann is a registered trademark of Reed Educational & Professional Publishing Ltd.

OXFORD FLORENCE PRAGUE MADRID ATHENS
MELBOURNE AUCKLAND KUALA LUMPUR SINGAPORE TOKYO
IBADAN NAIROBI KAMPALA JOHANNESBURG GABORONE
PORTSMOUTH NH CHICAGO MEXICO CITY SAO PAULO

Editor: Alyson Jones Designer: Nick Avery
Picture Researcher: Liz Eddison Art Director: Cathy Tincknell
Printed and bound in Italy. See-through pages printed by SMIC, France.

02 01 00 99 98
10 9 8 7 6 5 4 3 2 1

ISBN 0 431 06550 0

British Library Cataloguing in Publication Data
Llewellyn, Claire, First look through cities
1. Cities and towns - Juvenile literature I. Title II. Cities 307.7'6

Acknowledgements
The Publishers would like to thank the following for permission to reproduce photographs: page 5: Tony Stone Worldwide © Paul Chesley;
page 6: ZEFA; pages 7, 8 and 15: ZEFA © A. Liesecke; page 10: Britstock-IFA © M. Gottschalk; page 12: Tony Stone Images © Robin Smith;
page 17: Tony Stone Images © Hiroyuki Matsumoto; page 18: © Pictor International; page 21: Trip © W Jacobs.

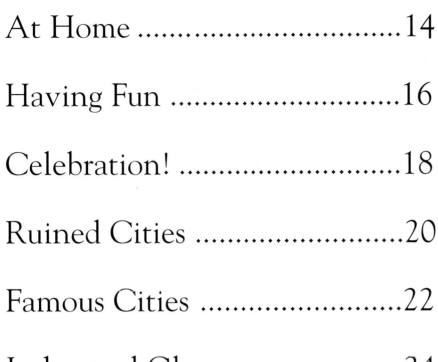

What is a City?

A **city** is a place where thousands of people live and work. Like towns, cities are made up of streets, parks and many different kinds of buildings. But cities are huge, and some can take hours to cross in a bus or car.

From the air, Paris, in France, is a patchwork of tall buildings, busy roads and green parkland. How many bridges can you see?

Every big city is packed with people. Some of them live there, but others are visiting or going to work.

Busy Streets

In the centre of the city there are banks, offices and the biggest shops. It's always busy here. Sometimes the streets are jam-packed with crowds of people shopping, or rushing to or from work.

Many cities now have huge shopping centres, with cafés and all kinds of shops.

People in a hurry can
pick up a quick snack to
eat from street sellers.
In Brazil this woman sells
vegetables and snacks.

High in the Sky

Cities are crowded places with little space to spare. To save land, people have built skyscrapers – towering buildings with dozens of different floors.

Some skyscrapers have over 5,000 windows. Look at the poor window-cleaners who have to clean them all!

New York's skyscrapers tower over the city. They look fabulous lit up at night.

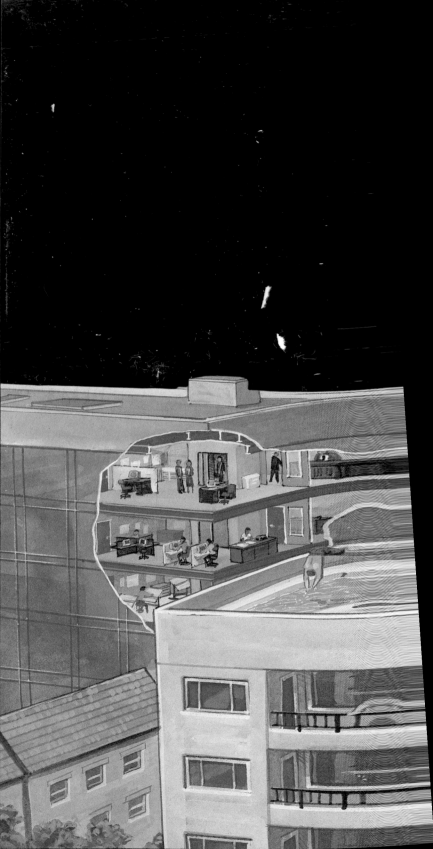

Inside each building there's
enough room for hundreds
of people to live or work.
There are plenty of stairways,
lifts, toilets and phones.

Work in the City

Outside the city centre people work in large factories making cars, computers and many different kinds of goods.

In the factories, skilled workers make the goods quickly and cheaply.

Every city on the coast has a port, where the goods are loaded onto ships. Singapore has one of the biggest ports in the world – over 100 ships dock here every day.

All week, the goods are packed onto trucks and trains, and delivered all over the country. Roads are carefully planned. They carry traffic in and out of the city centre as quickly as possible.

On the Move

People are always travelling from one part of a city to another. It's easy to jump on a bus or tram. Some cities have underground trains that make travelling even quicker.

How many different kinds of transport can you see in this Indian city?

Public transport, such as buses, trams and trains, helps to keep the city moving. Without it, many cities would be jammed with cars.

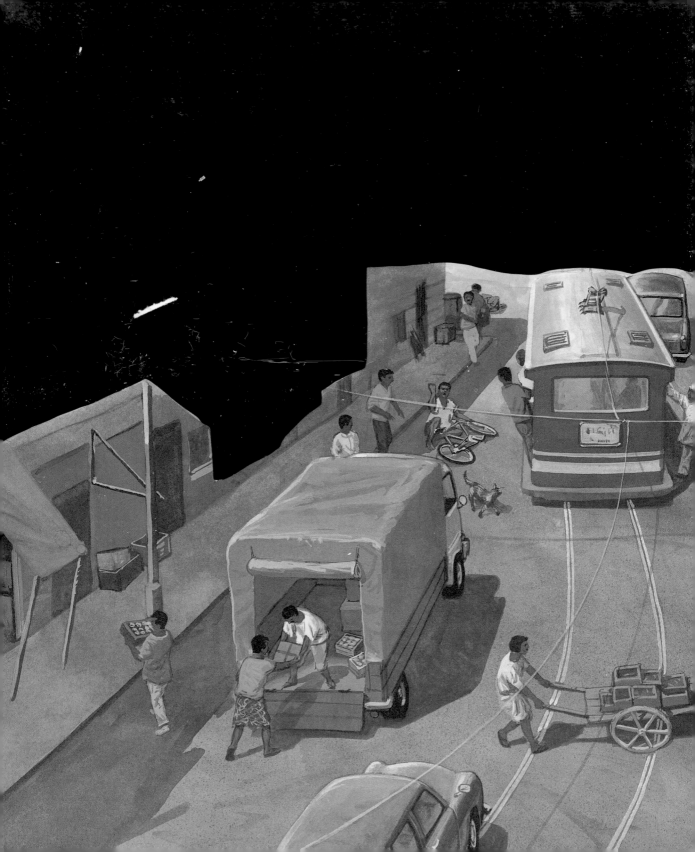

In Sydney, Australia, a monorail carries passengers above the streets. It's clean, quiet and gives a good view.

At Home

There are different kinds of homes in a city. Some people live in flats in the city centre, near to the cafés and shops. Other people live further out. They have a longer journey home, but their houses are bigger and have gardens, too.

You find tower blocks in every city. They are a way of squeezing a lot of homes into a very small space.

Sometimes there are not enough homes for everyone in some cities. The poorest people live in tumble-down shacks.

Having Fun

There's plenty to see and do in a city. You may be able to visit a palace, climb a tower, or cheer on your team at a sports match.

Some cities are by the sea. Behind the beach is a wide promenade, lined with palm trees, cafés and shops. There may even be a funfair!

Central Park lies at the heart of America's New York City. This huge green space is the perfect place to picnic in summer or ice-skate in winter.

Many people visit cities for their museums and art galleries. What kind of museum is this?

Celebration!

Now and again every city has special days, when it lets down its hair and has a party. Crowds gather on the streets to welcome a visitor, watch a parade, or celebrate something that happened a long time ago.

February is carnival time in Rio de Janeiro, Brazil. There are glittering parades, bright costumes – and music!

Bastille Day is an important French holiday. The city of Paris celebrates in style!

Cities in China celebrate their New Year with a dragon dance in the streets. Can you see the legs of the people inside the dragon?

Ruined Cities

Cities are not a new idea. People have been living and working in cities for thousands of years. Some of them have grown into the huge modern cities of today. Others are empty ruins, where grass grows in between the stones.

Athens in Greece has been a busy city for more than 2,500 years. You can still visit many of its ancient buildings.

The ruined city of Machu Picchu lies high in the mountains of Peru. The city was abandoned when the Spanish invaded over 450 years ago.

In some cities, like Mecca in Saudi Arabia, ancient buildings stand among modern shops and towers.

Famous Cities

Many of the world's cities have become famous for their beauty and history, and for certain buildings that are landmarks around the world. Do you recognise any in the pictures?

d.

a.

b.

c.

e.

f.

g.

h.

a. Houses of Parliament, London, UK
b. Taj Mahal, Agra, India
c. Leaning Tower, Pisa, Italy
d. The Kremlin, Moscow, Russia
e. The Opera House, Sydney, Australia
f. Statue of Christ, Rio de Janeiro, Brazil
g. Statue of Liberty, New York, USA
h. Eiffel Tower, Paris, France

Index

Glossary

Art gallery a public building where paintings are on display

Factory a building where goods are made

Flat a home on one floor of a large building

Invader someone who enters a city or country to attack it

Landmark a well-known building, monument or bridge

Monorail a railway with a single rail

Port a safe place for ships to dock (sail in and tie up)

Promenade a walkway along the coast in a holiday city

Public transport a way of carrying paying passengers from one place to another

Skyscraper a very tall city building

Traditional something that has been handed down from the past

Tram a vehicle that runs along metal rails in the road